The
Official Rules of
Soccer

www.ussoccer.com

TRIUMPH
BOOKS
CHICAGO

Cover photo of Chris Armas courtesy of
   John Todd/International Sports Images
Typography: Sue Knopf
Cover design by Patricia Frey

This book is available in quantity at special discounts for your group or organization. For further information contact:

Triumph Books
601 South LaSalle Street
Chicago, IL 60605
312-939-3330
FAX 312-663-3557

Printed in Canada
ISBN: 1-57243-693-X

Contents

Laws of the Game

User's Guide

This edition of the Official Laws of the Game has been designed to give soccer fans of all ages a quick and easy reference guide to the action on the field.

Diagrams illustrating offside points and signals by the referee and linesmen can all be found here following the Laws themselves.

Please note that any modifications to these rules are subject to the agreement of the National Associations as specified on the Notes page.

Notes on the Laws of the Game

Modifications

Subject to the agreement of the national association concerned and provided the principles of these Laws are maintained, the Laws may be modified in their application for matches for players of under 16 years of age, for women footballers, for veteran footballers (over 35 years) and for players with disabilities.

Any or all of the following modifications are permissible:

• size of the field of play

• size, weight and material of the ball

• width between the goalposts and height of the crossbar from the ground

• duration of the periods of play

• substitutions

Further modifications are only allowed with the consent of the International Football Association Board.

Male and Female

References to the male gender in the Laws of the Game in respect to referees, assistant referees, players and officials are for simplification and apply to both males and females.

Key

Throughout the Laws of the Game the following symbols are used:

* Unless covered by Special Circumstances listed in Law 8—The Start and Restart of Play

Shading indicates new Law changes

Law 1
The Field of Play

Field Surface

Matches may be played on natural or artificial surfaces, according to the rules of the competition.

Dimensions

The field of play must be rectangular. The length of the touch line must be greater than the length of the goal line.

Length: minimum 100 yds (90 m)
maximum 130 yds (120 m)

Width: minimum 50 yds (45 m)
maximum 100 yds (90 m)

International Matches

Length: minimum 110 yds (100 m)
maximum 120 yds (110 m)

Width: minimum 70 yds (64 m)
maximum 80 yds (75 m)

Field Markings

The field of play is marked with lines. These lines belong to the areas of which they are boundaries.

The two longer boundary lines are called touch lines. The two shorter lines are called goal lines.

All lines are not more than 5 ins (12 cm) wide.

The field of play is divided into two halves by a halfway line.

The center mark is indicated at the midpoint of the halfway line. A circle with a radius of 10 yds (9.15 m) is marked around it.

The Goal Area

A goal area is defined at each end of the field as follows:

Two lines are drawn at right angles to the goal line, 6 yds (5.5 m) from the inside of each goalpost. These lines extend into the field of play for a distance of 6 yds (5.5 m) and are joined by a line drawn parallel with the goal line. The area bounded by these lines and the goal line is the goal area.

The Penalty Area

A penalty area is defined at each end of the field as follows:

Two lines are drawn at right angles to the goal line, 18 yds (16.5 m) from the inside of each goalpost. These lines extend into the field of play for a distance of 18 yds (16.5 m) and are joined by a line drawn parallel with the goal line. The area bounded by these lines and the goal line is the penalty area.

Within each penalty area a penalty mark is made 12 yds (11 m) from the midpoint between the goalposts and equidistant to them. An arc of a circle with a radius of 10 yds (9.15 m) from each penalty mark is drawn outside the penalty area.

Flagposts

A flagpost, not less than 5 ft (1.5 m) high, with a non-pointed top and flag is placed at each corner.

Flagposts may also be placed at each end of the halfway line, not less than 1 yd (1 m) outside the touch line.

The Corner Arc

A quarter circle with a radius of 1 yd (1 m) from each corner flagpost is drawn inside the field of play.

The Field of Play

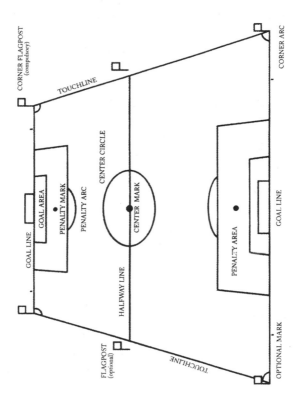

Measurements

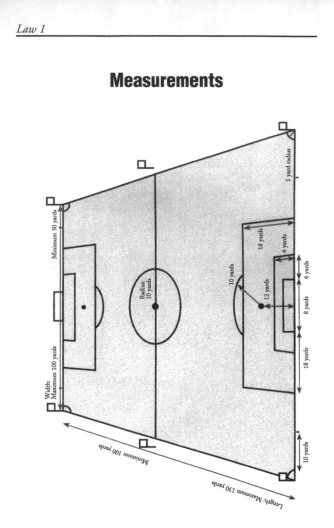

Corner Flagpost

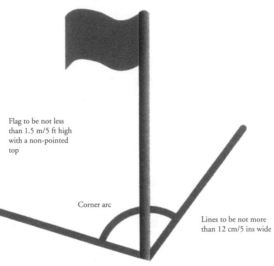

Flag to be not less than 1.5 m/5 ft high with a non-pointed top

Corner arc

Lines to be not more than 12 cm/5 ins wide

Corner flagpost is compulsory

Goals

Goals must be placed on the center of each goal line.

They consist of two upright posts equidistant from the corner flagposts and joined at the top by a horizontal crossbar.

The distance between the posts is 8 yds (7.32 m) and the distance from the lower edge of the crossbar to the ground is 8 ft (2.44 m).

Both goalposts and the crossbar have the same width and depth which do not exceed 5 ins (12 cm). The goal lines are the same width as that of the goalposts and the crossbar. Nets may be attached to the goals and the ground behind the goal, provided that they are properly supported and do not interfere with the goalkeeper.

The goalposts and crossbars must be white.

Safety

Goals must be anchored securely to the ground. Portable goals may only be used if they satisfy this requirement.

Decisions of the International F.A. Board

Decision 1
If the crossbar becomes displaced or broken, play is stopped until it has been repaired or replaced in position. If a repair is not possible, the match is abandoned. The use of a rope to replace the crossbar is not permitted. If the crossbar can be repaired, the match is restarted with a dropped ball at the place where the ball was located when play was stopped.* (see page v)

Decision 2
Goalposts and crossbars must be made of wood, metal or other approved material. Their shape may be square, rectangular, round or elliptical and they must not be dangerous to players.

Decision 3
No kind of commercial advertising, whether real or virtual, is permitted on the field of play and field equipment (including the goal nets and the areas they enclose) from the time the teams enter the field of play until they have left it at half-time and from the time the teams re-enter the field of play until the end of the match. In particular, no advertising material of any kind may be displayed on goals, nets, flagposts or their flags. No extraneous equipment (cameras, microphones, etc.) may be attached to these items.

Decision 4
There shall be no advertising of any kind within the technical area or within one metre from the touch line and outside the field play on the ground. Further, no advertising shall be allowed in the area between the goal line and the goal nets.

Decision 5
The reproduction, whether real or virtual, of representative logos or emblems of FIFA, confederations, national associations, leagues, clubs or other bodies, is forbidden on the field of play and field equipment (including the goal nets and the areas they enclose) during playing time, as described in Decision 3.

Decision 6
A mark may be made off the field of play, 10 yds (9.15 m) from the corner arc and at right angles to the goal lines to ensure that this distance is observed when a corner kick is being taken.

New International FA Board Decision 7
Where artificial surfaces are used in either competition matches between representative teams of associations affiliated to FIFA or international club competition matches, the surface must meet the requirements of the FIFA Quality Concept for Artificial Turf or the International Artificial Turf Standard, unless special dispensation is given by FIFA.

New International FA Board Decision 8
Where a technical area exists, it must meet the requirements approved by the International FA Board, which are contained in this publication.

Law 2
The Ball

Qualities and Measurements

The ball is:

- spherical

- made of leather or other suitable material

- of a circumference of not more than 28 ins (70 cm) and not less than 27 ins (68 cm)

- not more than 16 oz (450g) in weight and not less than 14 oz (410 g) at the start of the match

- of a pressure equal to 600-1100 g/cm2 (0.6-1.1 atmosphere) at sea level (8.5 lbs/sq in-15.6 lbs/sq in)

Replacement of a Defective Ball

If the ball bursts or becomes defective during the course of a match:

- the match is stopped

- the match is restarted by dropping the replacement ball at the place where the first ball became defective* (see page v)

If the ball bursts or becomes defective whilst not in play at a kick-off, goal kick, corner kick, free kick, penalty kick or throw-in:

- the match is restarted accordingly

The ball may not be changed during the match without the authority of the referee.

Decisions of the International F.A. Board

Decision 1

In competition matches, only footballs which meet the minimum technical requirements stipulated in Law 2 are permitted for use.

In FIFA competition matches, and in competition matches organized under the auspices of the confederations, acceptance of a football for use is conditional upon the football bearing one of the following three designations: the official "FIFA APPROVED" logo, the official "FIFA INSPECTED" logo, or the reference "INTERNATIONAL MATCHBALL STANDARD."

Such a designation on a football indicates that it has been tested officially and found to be in compliance with specific technical requirements, different for each category and additional to the minimum specifications stipulated in Law 2. The list of the additional requirements specific to each of the respective categories must be approved by the International F.A. Board. The institutes conducting the tests are subject to the approval of FIFA.

National association competitions may require the use of balls bearing any one of these three designations.

In all other matches the ball used must satisfy the requirements of Law 2.

Decision 2

In FIFA competition matches and in competition matches organized under the auspices of the confederations and national associations, no kind of commercial advertising on the ball is permitted, except for the emblem of the competition, the competition organizer and the authorized trademark of the manufacturer. The competition regulations may restrict the size and number of such markings.

Law 3
The Number
of Players

Players

A match is played by two teams, each consisting of not more than eleven players, one of whom is the goalkeeper. A match may not start if either team consists of fewer than seven players.

Official Competitions

Up to a maximum of three substitutes may be used in any match played in an official competition organized under the auspices of FIFA, the confederations or the national associations.

The rules of the competition must state how many substitutes may be nominated, from three up to a maximum of seven.

Other Matches

In other matches, up to six substitutes may be used.

All Matches

In all matches the names of the substitutes must be given to the referee prior to the start of the match. Substitutes not so named may not take part in the match.

Substitution Procedure

To replace a player by a substitute, the following conditions must be observed:

- the referee is informed before any proposed substitution is made

- a substitute only enters the field of play after the player being replaced has left and after receiving a signal from the referee.

- a substitute only enters the field of play at the halfway line and during a stoppage in the match

- a substitution is completed when a substitute enters the field of play

- from that moment, the substitute becomes a player and the player he has replaced ceases to be a player

- a player who has been replaced takes no further part in the match

- all substitutes are subject to the authority and jurisdiction of the referee, whether called upon to play or not

Changing the Goalkeeper

Any of the other players may change places with the goalkeeper, provided that:

- the referee is informed before the change is made

- the change is made during a stoppage in the match

Infringements/Sanctions

If a substitute enters the field of play without the referee's permission:

- play is stopped

- the substitute is cautioned, shown the yellow card and required to leave the field of play

- play is restarted with a dropped ball at the place it was located when play was stopped* (see page v)

If a player changes places with the goalkeeper without the referee's permission before the change is made:

- play continues

- the players concerned are cautioned and shown the yellow card when the ball is next out of play

For any other infringements of this Law:

- the players concerned are cautioned and shown the yellow card

---

Restart of Play

If play is stopped by the referee to administer a caution:

- the match is restarted by an indirect free kick, to be taken by a player of the opposing team from the place where the ball was located when play was stopped* (see page v)

Players and Substitutes Sent Off

A player who has been sent off before the kick-off may be replaced only by one of the named substitutes.

A named substitute who has been sent off, either before the kick-off or after play has started, may not be replaced.

Decisions of the International F.A. Board

Decision 1
Subject to the overriding conditions of Law 3, the minimum number of players in a team is left to the discretion of national associations. The Board is of the opinion, however, that a match should not continue if there are fewer than seven players in either team.

Decision 2
A team official may convey tactical instructions to the players during the match; he must return to his position after giving these instructions. All officials must remain within the confines of the technical area, where such an area is provided, and they must behave in a responsible manner.

Law 4
The Players'
Equipment

Safety

A player must not use equipment or wear anything which is dangerous to himself or another player (including any kind of jewelry).

Basic Equipment

The basic compulsory equipment of a player is:

- a jersey or shirt
- shorts—if thermal undershorts are worn, they are of the same main color as the shorts
- stockings
- shinguards
- footwear

Shinguards

- are covered entirely by the stockings
- are made of a suitable material (rubber, plastic or similar substances)
- provide a reasonable degree of protection

Goalkeepers

- each goalkeeper wears colors which distinguish him from the other players, the referee and the assistant referees

Infringements/Sanctions

For any infringement of this Law:

- play need not be stopped
- the player at fault is instructed by the referee to leave the field of play to correct his equipment
- the player leaves the field of play when the ball next ceases to be in play, unless he has already corrected his equipment

- any player required to leave the field of play to correct his equipment does not re-enter without the referee's permission
- the referee checks that the player's equipment is correct before allowing him to re-enter the field of play
- the player is only allowed to re-enter the field of play when the ball is out of play

A player who has been required to leave the field of play because of an infringement of this Law and who enters (or re-enters) the field of play without the referee's permission is cautioned and shown the yellow card.

Restart of Play

If play is stopped by the referee to administer a caution:

- the match is restarted by an indirect free kick taken by a player of the opposing side, from the place where the ball was located when the referee stopped the match* (see page v)

Decisions of the International F.A. Board

Decision 1

- Advertising is permitted only on the players' jerseys. It may not be worn on shorts, stockings or footwear.

- Players must not reveal undershirts that contain slogans or advertising. A player removing his jersey to reveal slogans or advertising will be sanctioned by the competition organizer.

- Jerseys must have sleeves.

Law 5
The Referee

The Authority of the Referee

Each match is controlled by a referee who has full authority to enforce the Laws of the Game in connection with the match to which he has been appointed.

Powers and Duties

The Referee:

- enforces the Laws of the Game

- controls the match in co-operation with the assistant referees and, where applicable, with the fourth official

- ensures that any ball used meets the requirements of Law 2

- ensures that the player's equipment meets the requirements of Law 4

- acts as timekeeper and keeps a record of the match

- stops, suspends or terminates the match, at his discretion, for any infringements of the Laws

- stops, suspends or terminates the match because of outside interference of any kind

- stops the match if, in his opinion, a player is seriously injured, and ensures that he is removed from the field of play. An injured player may only return to the field of play after the match has restarted.

- allows play to continue until the ball is out of play if a player is, in his opinion, only slightly injured

- ensures that any player bleeding from a wound leaves the field of play. The player may only return on receiving a signal from the referee, who must be satisfied that the bleeding has stopped

- allows play to continue when the team against which an offense has been committed will benefit from such an advantage and penalizes the original offense if the anticipated advantage does not ensue at that time

- punishes the more serious offense when a player commits more than one offense at the same time

- takes disciplinary action against players guilty of cautionable and sending-off offenses. He is not obliged to take this action immediately but must do so when the ball next goes out of play

- takes action against team officials who fail to conduct themselves in a responsible manner and may at his discretion, expel them from the field of play and its immediate surrounds

- acts on the advice of assistant referees regarding incidents which he has not seen

- ensures that no unauthorized persons enter the field of play

- restarts the match after it has been stopped

- provides the appropriate authorities with a match report which includes information on any disciplinary action taken against players, and/or team officials and any other incidents which occurred before, during or after the match

Decisions of the Referee

The decisions of the referee regarding facts connected with play are final.

The referee may only change a decision on realizing that it is incorrect or, at his discretion, on the advice of an assistant referee, provided that he has not restarted play.

Decisions of the International F.A. Board

Decision 1

A referee (or where applicable, an assistant referee or fourth official) is not held liable for:

• any kind of injury suffered by a player, official or spectator

• any damage to property of any kind

• any other loss suffered by any individual, club, company, associations or other body, which is due or which may be due to any decision which he may take under the terms of the Laws of the Game or in respect of the normal procedures required to hold, play and control a match.

This may include:

• a decision that the condition of the field of play or its surrounds or that the weather conditions are such as to allow or not to allow a match to take place

• a decision to abandon a match for whatever reason

• a decision as to the condition of the fixtures or equipment used during a match including the goalposts, crossbar, flagposts and the ball

• a decision to stop or not to stop a match due to spectator interference or any problem in the spectator area

• a decision to stop or not to stop play to allow an injured player to be removed from the field of play for treatment

• a decision to request or insist that an injured player be removed from the field of play for treatment

• a decision to allow or not to allow a player to wear certain apparel or equipment

• a decision (in so far as this may be his responsibility) to allow or not to allow any persons (including team or stadium officials, security officers, photographers or other media representatives) to be present in the vicinity of the field of play

• any other decision which he may take in accordance with the Laws of the Game or in conformity with his duties under the terms of FIFA, confederation, national association or league rules or regulations under which the match is played

International FA Board Decision 2
In tournaments or competitions where a fourth official is appointed, his role and duties must be in accordance with the guidelines approved by the International FA Board, which are contained in this publication.

Decision 3
Facts connected with play shall include whether a goal is scored or not and the result of the match.

Law 6
The Assistant
Referees

Duties

Two assistant referees are appointed whose duties, subject to the decision of the referee, are to indicate:

- when the whole of the ball has passed out of the field of play

- which side is entitled to a corner kick, goal kick or throw-in

- when a player may be penalized for being in an offside position

- when a substitution is requested

- when offences have been committed whenever the assistants are closer to the action than the referee (this includes, in particular circumstances, offences committed in the penalty area)

- whether, at penalty kicks, the goalkeeper has moved forward before the ball has been kicked and if the ball has crossed the line

Assistance

The assistant referees also assist the referee to control the match in accordance with the Laws of the Game. In particular, they may enter the field of play to help control the 9.15 m distance.

In the event of undue interference or improper conduct, the referee will relieve an assistant referee of his duties and make a report to the appropriate authorities.

Law 7
The Duration
of the Match

Periods of Play

The match last two equal periods of 45 minutes, unless otherwise mutually agreed between the referee and the two participating teams. Any agreement to alter the periods of play (for example to reduce each half to 40 minutes because of insufficient light) must be made before the start of play and must comply with competition rules.

Half-Time Interval

Players are entitled to an interval at half-time.

The half-time interval must not exceed 15 minutes.

Competition rules must state the duration of the half-time interval.

The duration of the half-time interval may be altered only with the consent of the referee.

Allowance for Time Lost

Allowance is made in either period for all time lost through:

- substitution(s)
- assessment of injury to players
- removal of injured players from the field of play for treatment
- wasting time
- any other cause

The allowance for time lost is at the discretion of the referee.

Penalty Kick

Additional time is allowed for a penalty kick to be taken or retaken at the end of each half or at the end of periods of extra time.

Abandoned Match

An abandoned match is replayed unless the competition rules provide otherwise.

Law 8
The Start and
Restart of Play

Preliminaries

A coin is tossed and the team which wins the toss decides which goal it will attack in the first half of the match.

The other team takes the kick-off to start the match.

The team which wins the toss takes the kick-off to start the second half of the match.

In the second half of the match the teams change ends and attack the opposite goals.

Kick-off

A kick-off is a way of starting or restarting play:

- at the start of the match
- after a goal has been scored
- at the start of the second half of the match
- at the start of each period of extra time, where applicable

A goal may be scored directly from the kick-off.

Procedure

- all players are in their own half of the field
- the opponents of the team taking the kick-off are at least 10 yds (9.15 m) from the ball until it is in play
- the ball is stationary on the center mark
- the referee gives a signal
- the ball is in play when it is kicked and moves forward
- the kicker does not touch the ball a second time until it has touched another player

After a team scores a goal, the kick-off is taken by the other team.

Infringements/Sanctions

If the kicker touches the ball a second time before it has touched another player:

- an indirect free kick is awarded to the opposing team to be taken from the place where the infringement occurred* (see page v)

For any other infringement of the kick-off procedure:

- the kick-off is retaken

Dropped Ball

A dropped ball is a way of restarting the match after a temporary stoppage which becomes necessary, while the ball is in play, for any reason not mentioned elsewhere in the Laws of the Game.

Procedure

The referee drops the ball at the place where it was located when play was stopped.* (see page v)

Play restarts when the ball touches the ground.

Infringements/Sanctions

The ball is dropped again:

- if it is touched by a player before it makes contact with the ground

- if the ball leaves the field of play after it makes contact with the ground, without a player touching it

---

Special Circumstances

A free kick awarded to the defending team inside its own goal area is taken from any point within the goal area.

An indirect free kick awarded to the attacking team in its opponents' goal area is taken from the goal area line parallel to the goal line at the point nearest to where the infringement occurred.

A dropped ball to restart the match after play has been temporarily stopped inside the goal area takes place on the goal area line parallel to the goal line at the point nearest to where the ball was located when play was stopped.

Law 9
The Ball In
and Out of Play

Ball Out of Play

The ball is out of play when:

- it has wholly crossed the goal line or touch line whether on the ground or in the air

- play has been stopped by the referee

Ball In Play

The ball is in play at all other times, including when:

- it rebounds from a goalpost, crossbar, or corner flagpost and remains in the field of play

- it rebounds from either the referee or an assistant referee when they are on the field of play

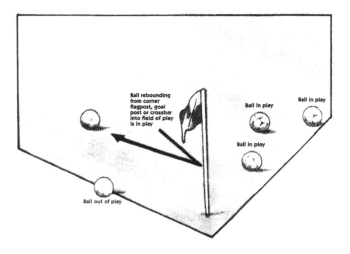

Ball rebounding from corner flagpost, goal post or crossbar into field of play is in play

Ball in play

Ball in play

Ball in play

Ball out of play

Law 10
The Method
of Scoring

Goal Scored

A goal is scored when the whole of the ball passes over the goal line, between the goalposts and under the crossbar, provided that no infringement of the Laws of the Game has been committed previously by the team scoring the goal.

Winning Team

The team scoring the greater number of goals during a match is the winner. If both teams score an equal number of goals, or if no goals are scored, the match is drawn.

Competition Rules

When competition rules require there to be a winning team after a match has been drawn, only the following procedures, which have been approved by the International FA Board, are permitted:

* away goals rule

* extra time

* kicks from the penalty mark

New International FA Board Decision 1
Only procedures to determine the winner of a match, which are approved by the International FA Board and contained in this publication, are permitted in competition rules.

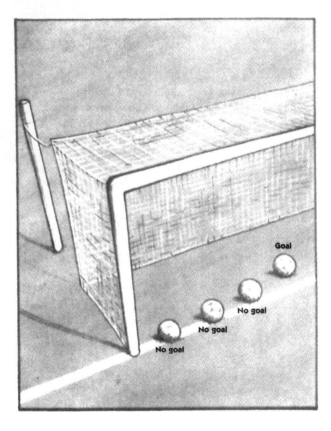

Law 11
Offside

Offside Position

It is not an offense in itself to be in an offside position.

A player is in an offside position if:

- he is nearer to his opponents' goal line than both the ball and the second last opponent

A player is not in an offside position if:

- he is in his own half of the field of play, or
- he is level with the second last opponent, or
- he is level with the last two opponents

Offense

A player in an offside position is only penalized if, at the moment the ball touches or is played by one of his team, he is, in the opinion of the referee, involved in active play by:

- interfering with play, or
- interfering with an opponent, or
- gaining an advantage by being in that position

No Offense

There is no offside offense if a player receives the ball directly from:

- a goal kick, or
- a throw-in, or
- a corner kick

Infringements/Sanctions

For any offside offense, the referee awards an indirect free kick to the opposing team to be taken from the place where the infringement occurred* (see page v)

Law 12
Fouls and
Misconduct

Fouls and misconduct are penalized as follows:

Direct Free Kick

A direct free kick is awarded to the opposing team if a player commits any of the following six offenses in a manner considered by the referee to be careless, reckless or using excessive force:

- kicks or attempts to kick an opponent
- trips or attempts to trip an opponent
- jumps at an opponent
- charges an opponent
- strikes or attempts to strike an opponent
- pushes an opponent

A direct free kick is also awarded to the opposing team if a player commits any of the following four offenses:

- tackles an opponent to gain possession of the ball, making contact with the opponent before touching the ball
- holds an opponent
- spits at an opponent
- handles the ball deliberately (except for the goalkeeper within his own penalty area)

A direct free kick is taken from where the offense occurred.*
(see page v)

Penalty Kick

A penalty kick is awarded if any of the above ten offenses is committed by a player inside his own penalty area, irrespective of the position of the ball, provided it is in play.

Indirect Free Kick

An indirect free kick is awarded to the opposing team if a goalkeeper, inside his own penalty area, commits any of the following four offenses:

- takes more than four steps while controlling the ball with his hands, before releasing it from his possession

- touches the ball again with his hands after it has been released from his possession and has not touched any other player

- touches the ball with his hands after it has been deliberately kicked to him by a team-mate

- touches the ball with his hands after he has received it directly from a throw-in taken by a team-mate

An indirect free kick is also awarded to the opposing team if a player, in the opinion of the referee:

- plays in a dangerous manner

- impedes the progress of an opponent

- prevents the goalkeeper from releasing the ball from his hands

- commits any other offense, not previously mentioned in Law 12, for which play is stopped to caution or dismiss a player

The indirect free kick is taken from where the offense occurred.* (see page v)

Disciplinary Sanctions

Only a player or substitute or substituted player may be shown the red or yellow card.

Cautionable Offenses

A player is cautioned and shown the yellow card if he commits any of the following seven offenses:

1. is guilty of unsporting behavior

2. shows dissent by word or action

3. persistently infringes the Laws of the Game

4. delays the restart of play

5. fails to respect the required distance when play is restarted with a corner kick or free kick

6. enters or re-enters the field of play without the referee's permission

7. deliberately leaves the field of play without the referee's permission

Sending-Off Offenses

A player is sent off and shown the red card if he commits any of the following seven offenses:

1. is guilty of serious foul play

2. is guilty of violent conduct

3. spits at an opponent or any other person

---

4. denies the opposing team a goal or an obvious goal-scoring opportunity by deliberately handling the ball (this does not apply to a goalkeeper within his own penalty area)

5. denies an obvious goal-scoring opportunity to an opponent moving towards the player's goal by an offense punishable by a free kick or a penalty kick

6. uses offensive, insulting or abusive language and/or gestures

7. receives a second caution in the same match

A player who has been sent off must leave the vicinity of the field of play and the technical area.

Decisions of the International F.A. Board

Decision 1
A player who commits a cautionable or sending-off offense, either on or off the field of play, whether directed towards an opponent, a team-mate, the referee, an assistant referee or any other person, is disciplined according to the nature of the offense committed.

Decision 2
The goalkeeper is considered to be in control of the ball by touching it with any part of his hand or arms. Possession of the ball includes the goalkeeper deliberately parrying the ball, but does not include the circumstances where, in the opinion of the referee, the ball rebounds accidentally from the goalkeeper, for example after he has made a save.

Decision 3
Subject to the terms of Law 12, a player may pass the ball to his own goalkeeper using his head or chest or knee, etc. If, however, in the opinion of the referee, a player uses a deliberate trick while the ball is in play in order to circumvent the Law, the player is guilty of unsporting behavior. He is cautioned, shown the yellow card and an indirect free kick is awarded to the opposing team from the place where the infringement occurred.* (see page v)

A player using a deliberate trick to circumvent the Law while he is taking a free kick, is cautioned for unsporting behavior and shown the yellow card. The free kick is retaken.

In such circumstances, it is irrelevant whether the goalkeeper subsequently touches the ball with his hands or not. The offense is committed by the player in attempting to circumvent both the letter and the spirit of Law 12.

Decision 4
A tackle from behind, which endangers the safety of an opponent, must be sanctioned as serious foul play.

Decision 5
Any simulating action anywhere on the field, which is intended to deceive the referee, must be sanctioned as unsporting behavior.

New International FA Board Decision 6
A player who removes his jersey when celebrating a goal must be cautioned for unsporting behavior.

Law 13
Free Kicks

Types of Free Kicks

Free kicks are either direct or indirect.

For both direct and indirect free kicks, the ball must be stationary when the kick is taken and the kicker does not touch the ball a second time until it has touched another player.

The Direct Free Kick

- if a direct free kick is kicked directly into the opponents' goal, a goal is awarded

- if a direct free kick is kicked directly into the team's own goal, a corner kick is awarded to the opposing team

The Indirect Free Kick

Signal

The referee indicates an indirect free kick by raising his arm above his head. He maintains his arm in that position until the kick has been taken and the ball has touched another player or goes out of play.

Ball Enters the Goal

A goal can be scored only if the ball subsequently touches another player before it enters the goal.

- if an indirect free kick is kicked directly into the opponents' goal, a goal kick is awarded

- if an indirect free kick is kicked directly into the team's own goal, a corner kick is awarded to the opposing team

Position of Free Kick

Free Kick Inside the Penalty Area

Direct or indirect free kick to the defending team:

- all opponents are at least 10 yds (9.15 m) from the ball
- all opponents remain outside the penalty area until the ball is in play
- the ball is in play when it is kicked directly beyond the penalty area
- a free kick awarded in the goal area is taken from any point inside that area

Indirect free kick to the attacking team:

- all opponents are at least 10 yds (9.15 m) from the ball until it is in play, unless they are on their own goal line between the goalposts
- the ball is in play when it is kicked and moves
- an indirect free kick awarded inside the goal area is taken from that part of the goal area line which runs parallel to the goal line, at the point nearest to where the infringement occurred

Free Kick Outside the Penalty Area

- all opponents are at least 10 yds (9.15 m) from the ball until it is in play
- the ball is in play when it is kicked and moves
- the free kick is taken from the place where the infringement occurred

Infringements/Sanctions

If, when a free kick is taken, an opponent is closer to the ball than the required distance:

• the kick is retaken

If, when a free kick is taken by the defending team from inside its own penalty area, the ball is not kicked directly into play:

• the kick is retaken

Free kick taken by a player other than the goalkeeper

If, after the ball is in play, the kicker touches the ball a second time (except with his hands) before it has touched another player:

• an indirect free kick is awarded to the opposing team, the kick to be taken from the place where the infringement occurred* (see page v)

If, after the ball is in play, the kicker deliberately handles the ball before it has touched another player:

• a direct free kick is awarded to the opposing team, the kick to be taken from the place where the infringement occurred* (see page v)

• a penalty kick is awarded if the infringement occurred inside the kicker's penalty area

Free kick taken by the goalkeeper
If, after the ball is in play, the goalkeeper touches the ball a second time (except with his hands), before it has touched another player:

- an indirect free kick is awarded to the opposing team, the kick to be taken from the place where the infringement occurred* (see page v)

If, after the ball is in play, the goalkeeper deliberately handles the ball before it has touched another player:

- a direct free kick is awarded to the opposing team if the infringement occurred outside the goalkeeper's penalty area, the kick to be taken from the place where the infringement occurred* (see page v)

- an indirect free kick is awarded to the opposing team if the infringement occurred inside the goalkeeper's penalty area, the kick to be taken from the place where the infringement occurred* (see page v)

Law 14
The Penalty Kick

A penalty kick is awarded against a team which commits one of the ten offenses for which a direct free kick is awarded, inside its own penalty area and while the ball is in play.

A goal may be scored directly from a penalty kick.

Additional time is allowed for a penalty kick to be taken at the end of each half or at the end of periods of extra time.

Position of the Ball and the Players

The ball:

- is placed on the penalty mark

The player taking the penalty kick:

- is properly identified

The defending goalkeeper:

- remains on his goal line, facing the kicker, between the goalposts until the ball has been kicked

The players other than the kicker are located:

- inside the field of play
- outside the penalty area
- behind the penalty mark
- at least 10 yds (9.15 m) from the penalty mark

The referee:

- does not signal for a penalty kick to be taken until the players have taken up position in accordance with the Law
- decides when a penalty kick has been completed

Procedure

- the player taking the penalty kicks the ball forward
- he does not play the ball a second time until it has touched another player
- the ball is in play when it is kicked and moves forward

When a penalty kick is taken during the normal course of play, or time has been extended at half-time or full time to allow a penalty kick to be taken or retaken, a goal is awarded if, before passing between the goalposts and under the crossbar:

- the ball touches either or both of the goalposts and/or crossbar, and/or the goalkeeper

---

Infringements/Sanctions

If the referee gives the signal for a penalty kick to be taken and, before the ball is in play, one of the following situations occurs:

The player taking the penalty kick infringes the Laws of the Game:

- the referee allows the kick to proceed
- if the ball enters the goal, the kick is retaken
- if the ball does not enter the goal, the kick is not retaken

The goalkeeper infringes the Laws of the Game:

- the referee allows the kick to proceed
- if the ball enters the goal, a goal is awarded

- if the ball does not enter the goal, the kick is retaken

A team-mate of the player taking the kick enters the penalty area or moves in front of or within 10 yds (9.15 m) of the penalty mark:

- the referee allows the kick to proceed
- if the ball enters the goal, the kick is retaken
- if the ball does not enter the goal, the kick is not retaken
- if the ball rebounds from the goalkeeper, the crossbar or the goalpost and is touched by this player, the referee stops play and restarts the match with an indirect free kick to the defending team

A team-mate of the goalkeeper enters the penalty area or moves in front of or within 10 yds (9.15 m) of the penalty mark:

- the referee allows the kick to proceed
- if the ball enters the goal, a goal is awarded
- if the ball does not enter the goal, the kick is retaken

A player of both the defending team and the attacking team infringes the Laws of the Game:

- the kick is retaken

If, after the penalty kick has been taken:

The kicker touches the ball a second time (except with his hands) before it has touched another player:

- an indirect free kick is awarded to the opposing team, the kick to be taken from the place where the infringement occurred* (see page v)

The kicker deliberately handles the ball before it has touched another player:

- a direct free kick is awarded to the opposing team, the kick to be taken from the place where the infringement occurred* (see page v)

The ball is touched by an outside agent as it moves forward:

- the kick is retaken

The ball rebounds into the field of play from the goalkeeper, the crossbar or the goalposts, and is then touched by an outside agent:

- the referee stops play
- play is restarted with a dropped ball at the place where it touched the outside agent* (see page v)

Law 15
The Throw-In

A throw-in is a method of restarting play. A goal cannot be scored directly from a throw-in. A throw-in is awarded:

- when the whole of the ball passes over the touch line, either on the ground or in the air

- from the point where it crossed the touch line

- to the opponents of the player who last touched the ball

Procedure

At the moment of delivering the ball, the thrower:

- faces the field of play

- has part of each foot either on the touch line or on the ground outside the touch line

- uses both hands

- delivers the ball from behind and over his head

The thrower may not touch the ball again until it has touched another player. The ball is in play immediately when it enters the field of play.

Infringements/Sanctions

Throw-in taken by a player other than the goalkeeper

If, after the ball is in play, the thrower touches the ball a second time (except with his hands) before it has touched another player:

- an indirect free kick is awarded to the opposing team, the kick to be taken from the place where the infringement occurred* (see page v)

If, after the ball is in play, the thrower deliberately handles the ball before it has touched another player:

- a direct free kick is awarded to the opposing team, the kick to be taken from the place where the infringement occurred* (see page v)

- a penalty kick is awarded if the infringement occurred inside the thrower's penalty area

Throw-in taken by the goalkeeper

If, after the ball is in play, the goalkeeper touches the ball a second time (except with his hands), before it has touched another player:

- an indirect free kick is awarded to the opposing team, the kick to be taken from the place where the infringement occurred* (see page v)

If, after the ball is in play, the goalkeeper deliberately handles the ball before it has touched another player:

- a direct free kick is awarded to the opposing team if the infringement occurred outside the goalkeeper's penalty area, the kick to be taken from the place where the infringement occurred* (see page v)

- an indirect free kick is awarded to the opposing team if the infringement occurred inside the goalkeeper's penalty area, the kick to be taken from the place where the infringement occurred* (see page v)

If an opponent unfairly distracts or impedes the thrower:

- he is cautioned for unsporting behavior and shown the yellow card

For any other infringement of this Law:

- the throw-in is taken by a player of the opposing team

Law 16
The Goal Kick

A goal kick is a method of restarting play. A goal may be scored directly from a goal kick, but only against the opposing team. A goal kick is awarded when:

- the whole of the ball, having last touched a player of the attacking team, passes over the goal line, either on he ground or in the air, and a goal is not scored in accordance with Law 10

Procedure

- the ball is kicked from any point within the goal area by a player of the defending team
- opponents remain outside the penalty area until the ball is in play
- the kicker does not play the ball a second time until it has touched another player
- the ball is in play when it is kicked directly beyond the penalty area

Infringements/Sanctions

If the ball is not kicked directly into play beyond the penalty area:

- the kick is retaken

Goal kick taken by a player other than the goalkeeper

If, after the ball is in play, the kicker touches the ball a second time (except with his hands) before it has touched another player:

- an indirect free kick is awarded to the opposing team, the kick to be taken from the place where the infringement occurred* (see page v)

If, after the ball is in play, the kicker deliberately handles the ball before it has touched another player:

- a direct free kick is awarded to the opposing team, the kick to be taken from the place where the infringement occurred* (see page v)

- a penalty kick is awarded if the infringement occurred inside the kicker's penalty area

Goal kick taken by the goalkeeper

If, after the ball is in play, the goalkeeper touches the ball a second time (except with his hands) before it has touched another player:

- an indirect free kick is awarded to the opposing team, the kick to be taken from the place where the infringement occurred* (see page v)

If, after the ball is in play, the goalkeeper deliberately handles the ball before it has touched another player:

- a direct free kick is awarded to the opposing team if the infringement occurred outside the goalkeeper's penalty area, the kick to be taken from the place where the infringement occurred* (see page v)

- an indirect free kick is awarded to the opposing team if the infringement occurred inside the goalkeeper's penalty area, the kick to be taken from the placc where the infringement occurred* (see page v)

For any other infringement of this Law:

- the kick is retaken

Law 17
The Corner Kick

A corner kick is a method of restarting play. A goal may be scored directly from a corner kick, but only against the opposing team. A corner kick is awarded when:

- the whole of the ball, having last touched a player of the defending team, passes over the goal line, either on the ground or in the air, and a goal is not scored in accordance with Law 10

Procedure

- the ball is placed inside the corner arc at the nearest corner flagpost
- the corner flagpost is not moved
- opponents remain at least 10 yds (9.15 m) from the ball until it is in play
- the ball is kicked by a player of the attacking team
- the ball is in play when it is kicked and moves
- the kicker does not play the ball a second time until it has touched another player

---

Infringements/Sanctions

Corner kick taken by a player other than the goalkeeper

If, after the ball is in play, the kicker touches the ball a second time (except with his hands) before it has touched another player:

- an indirect free kick is awarded to the opposing team, the kick to be taken from the place where the infringement occurred* (see page v)

If, after the ball is in play, the kicker deliberately handles the ball before it has touched another player:

- a direct free kick is awarded to the opposing team, the kick to be taken from the place where the infringement occurred* (see page v)

- a penalty kick is awarded if the infringement occurred inside the kicker's penalty area

Corner kick taken by the goalkeeper

If, after the ball is in play, the goalkeeper touches the ball a second time (except with his hands) before it has touched another player:

- an indirect free kick is awarded to the opposing team, the kick to be taken from the place where the infringement occurred* (see page v)

If, after the ball is in play, the goalkeeper deliberately handles the ball before it has touched another player:

- a direct free kick is awarded to the opposing team if the infringement occurred outside the goalkeeper's penalty area, the kick to be taken from the place where the infringement occurred* (see page v)

- an indirect free kick is awarded to the opposing team if the infringement occurred inside the goalkeeper's penalty area, the kick to be taken from the place where the infringement occurred* (see page v)

For any other infringement:

- the kick is retaken

Appendix 1: Procedures to Determine the Winner of a Match

Procedures to Determine the Winner of a Match

Away goals, extra time and taking kicks from the penalty mark are methods of determining the winning team where competition rules require there to be a winning team after a match has been drawn.

Away Goals

Competition rules may provide that where teams play each other home and away, if the scores are equal after the second match, any goals scored at the ground of the opposing team will count double.

Extra Time

Competition rules may provide for two further equal periods, not exceeding 15 minutes each, to be played. The conditions of Law 8 will apply

Kicks from the Penalty Mark

Procedure

- The referee chooses the goal at which the kicks will be taken
- The referee tosses a coin and the team whose captain wins the toss decides whether to take the first or the second kick
- The referee keeps a record of the kicks being taken
- Subject to the conditions explained below, both teams take five kicks

- The kicks are taken alternately by the teams

- If, before both teams have taken five kicks, one has scored more goals than the other could score, even if it were to complete its five kicks, no more kicks are taken

- If, after both teams have taken five kicks, both have scored the same number of goals, or have not scored any goals, kicks continue to be taken in the same order until one team has scored a goal more than the other from the same number of kicks

- A goalkeeper who is injured while kicks are being taken from the penalty mark and is unable to continue as goalkeeper may be replaced by a named substitute provided his team has not used the maximum number of substitutes permitted under the competition rules

- With the exception of the foregoing case, only players who are on the field of play at the end of the match, which includes extra time where appropriate, are allowed to take kicks from the penalty mark

- Each kick is taken by a different player and all eligible players must take a kick before any player can take a second kick

- An eligible player may change places with the goalkeeper at any time when kicks from the penalty mark are being taken

- Only the eligible players and match officials are permitted to remain on the field of play when kicks from the penalty mark are being taken

- All players, except the player taking the kick and the two goalkeepers, must remain within the center circle

- The goalkeeper who is the team-mate of the kicker must remain on the field of play, outside the penalty area in which the kicks are being taken, on the goal line where it meets the penalty area boundary line.

- Unless otherwise stated, the relevant Laws of the Game and International F.A. Board Decisions apply when kicks from the penalty mark are being taken.

- When a team finishes the match with a greater number of players than their opponents, they shall reduce their numbers to equate with that of their opponents and inform the referee of the name and number of each player excluded. The team captain has this responsibility.

- Before the start of kicks from the penalty mark the referee shall ensure that only an equal number of players from each team remain within the center circle and they shall take the kicks.

Appendix 2:
The Technical Area and the Fourth Official

The Technical Area

The Technical Area

The technical area as described in Law 3, International F.A. Board Decision no. 2, relates particularly to matches played in stadia with a designated seated area for technical staff and substitutes as shown below.

Technical areas may vary between stadia, for example in size or location, and the following notes are issued for general guidance.

- The technical area extends 1 yd (1 m) on either side of the designated seated area and extends forward up to a distance of 1 yd (1 m) from the touch line.

- It is recommended that markings are used to define this area.

- The number of persons permitted to occupy the technical area is defined by the competition rules.

- The occupants of the technical area are identified before the beginning of the match in accordance with the competition rules.

- Only one person at a time is authorized to convey tactical instructions and he must return to his position immediately after giving these instructions.

- The coach and other officials must remain within the confines of the technical area except in special circumstances, for example, a physiotherapist or doctor entering the field of play, with the referee's permission, to assess an injured player.

- The coach and other occupants of the technical area must behave in a responsible manner.

The Fourth Official

- The fourth official may be appointed under the competition rules and officiates if any of the three match officials is unable to continue.

- Prior to start of the competition, the organizer states clearly whether, if the referee is unable to continue, the fourth official takes over as the match referee or whether the senior assistant referee takes over as referee with the fourth official becoming an assistant referee.

- The fourth official assists with any administrative duties before, during and after the match, as required by the referee.

- He is responsible for assisting with substitution procedures during the match.

- He supervises the replacement footballs, where required. If the match ball has to be replaced during a match, he provides another ball, on the instruction of the referee, thus keeping the delay to a minimum.

- He has the authority to check the equipment of substitutes before they enter the field of play. If their equipment does not comply with the Laws of the Game, he informs the referee.

- The fourth official assists the referee at all times. He must indicate to the referee when the wrong player is cautioned because of mistaken identity or when a player is not sent off having been seen to be given a second caution or when violent conduct occurs out of the view of the referee and assistant referees. The referee, however, retains the authority to decide on all points connected with play.

- After the match, the fourth official must submit a report to the appropriate authorities on any misconduct or other incident which has occurred out of the view of the referee and the assistant referees. The fourth official must advise the referee and his assistants of any report being made.

- He has the authority to inform the referee of irresponsible behavior by any occupant of the technical area.

Appendix 3:
Law 11 Diagrams

Diagram 1 – Offside: The attacker who receives the ball from his team-mate, number 9, is offside since he is nearer to his opponent's goal line than the ball and the second last defender and gains an advantage by being in that position.

Diagram 2 – Not Offside: The attacker who receives the ball from his team-mate, number 8, is not offside because, when the ball is kicked, he is level with the second last defender.

Diagram 3 – Not Offside: The attacker is not offside because, when the ball is played to him by his team-mate, number 7, he is level with the second last defender.

Diagram 4 – Not Offside: A player cannot be offside from a throw-in.

Diagram 5 – Offside: The attacker, number 9, is offside because he is involved in active play and is interfering with the goalkeeper.

Diagram 6 – Offside: The attacker, number 9, is offside because he is in an offside position and is interfering with the goalkeeper.

Diagram 7 – Not Offside: The player lying in the goal area is not offside since he is not involved in active play and is not interfering with the goalkeeper.

Diagram 8 – Not Offside: Although the attacker is in an offside position when the ball is kicked by his team-mate, number 10, he is not penalized because he is not involved in active play and does not gain an advantage by being in that position.

Diagram 9 – Offside: The shot by number 6 rebounds from the goalpost to a team-mate who is penalized for being in an offside position, because when the ball is played, he is involved in active play and gains an advantage by being in that position.

Diagram 10 – Offside: The shot by a team-mate rebounds from the goalkeeper to number 8 who is penalized for being in an offside position because, when the ball is played, he is involved in active play and gains an advantage by being in that position.

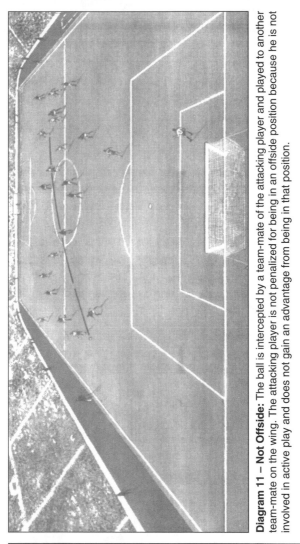

Diagram 11 – Not Offside: The ball is intercepted by a team-mate of the attacking player and played to another team-mate on the wing. The attacking player is not penalized for being in an offside position because he is not involved in active play and does not gain an advantage from being in that position.

Appendix 4:
Law 12 Diagrams

Diagram 1: The ball is played towards goal by the attacking team and a defender jumps and handles it as the attacking player moves towards the ball. The defender is sent off for denying the opposing team an obvious goal-scoring opportunity.

Diagram 2: The ball is played forward to an attacking player and the goalkeeper handles it outside the penalty area. The goalkeeper is sent off for denying the opposing team an obvious goal-scoring opportunity.

Diagram 3: An attacker, number 10, shoots the ball towards the goal. Just before it crosses the goal line into the goal a defender punches the ball over the bar. A penalty kick is awarded and the defender is sent off for denying the opposing team a goal.

Diagram 4: A defender intentionally handles the ball inside his own penalty area and the referee awards a penalty kick. He does not send off the defender since no obvious goal-scoring opportunity has been denied. If the ball strikes the defender accidentally, no offense is committed.

Diagram 5: The goalkeeper pulls down an attacking player inside his penalty area and a penalty kick is awarded. The goalkeeper is not sent off since the attacking player is moving away from the goal and does not have an obvious goal-scoring opportunity.

Diagram 6: An attacking player, number 10, is moving forward near the touch line when he is tripped by a defender. Number 10 does not have an obvious goal-scoring opportunity and so the defender is not sent off.

Diagram 7: An attacker is moving towards goal with an obvious goal-scoring opportunity when he is tripped by a defender. The defender is sent off for denying an opponent a goal-scoring opportunity.

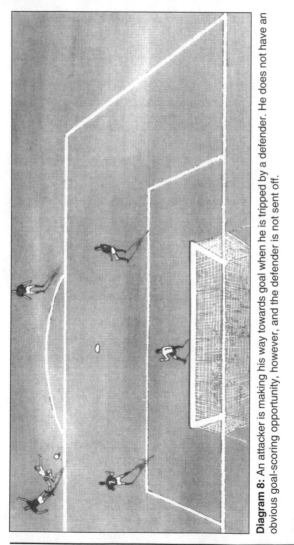

Diagram 8: An attacker is making his way towards goal when he is tripped by a defender. He does not have an obvious goal-scoring opportunity, however, and the defender is not sent off.

Diagram 9: An attacker is tripped by a defender inside the penalty area and a penalty kick is awarded. The defender is not sent off because the attacker is moving away from goal and does not have an obvious goal-scoring opportunity.

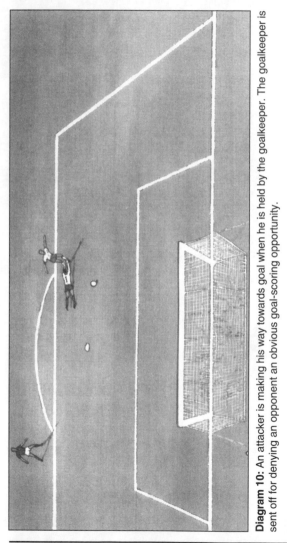

Diagram 10: An attacker is making his way towards goal when he is held by the goalkeeper. The goalkeeper is sent off for denying an opponent an obvious goal-scoring opportunity.

Appendix 5:
Referees and
Assistant Referees

Co-Operation Between the Referee and Assistant Referees— Law 6

In the Laws of the Game set out in the foregoing pages there are no instructions as to the relative positioning of the referee and assistant referees during a game. There are, however, instructions in Laws 5 and 6 with regard to the powers and duties of the referee and assistant referee which, rightly interpreted, imply co-operation. Law 6 stipulates that two assistant referees shall be appointed, whose duty (subject to the decision of the referee) shall be to:

(a) signal when the ball is out of play;

(b) signal when the ball has crossed the goal line and whether a corner kick or a goal kick is to be awarded;

(c) signal which side is entitled to the throw-in;

(d) assist the referee in conducting the game in accordance with the Laws.

The assistance referred to in (d) consists of:

1. signaling when the whole of the ball is out of play;

2. indicating which side is entitled to the corner kick, the goal kick, or the throw-in;

3. calling the attention of the referee to rough play or ungentlemanly conduct;

4. indicating to the referee when a substitution is desired;

5. giving an opinion on any point on which the referee may consult him.

Neutral assistant referees

The assistance referred to above is best given by neutral assistant referees. A limitation is placed upon club assistant referees because points 2., 3. and 4. are not usually referred to assistant referees who are not neutral. Neutral assistant referees must co-operate with the referee. In this case, the referee must adopt the appropriate attitude, because in effect there are three officials supervising play; the referee as principal official and the assistant referees to help him to control the game in a proper manner.

Club assistant referees

To acquire the most effective co-operation from club assistant referees, the following procedure shall be adopted:

1. Both club assistant referees shall report to the referee before the start of the match for instructions. He shall inform them that, regardless of their personal opinion, his decision is final and must not be questioned.

2. Their work as club assistant referees is to signal when the ball is entirely over the touch line and to indicate which side is entitled to the throw-in, subject always to the decision of the referee.

Keeping in mind their distinct duties as outlined above, the referee shall decide beforehand exactly what he requires of the club assistant referees and, as head of the trio, tell them clearly how they can best assist him. The three officials must therefore confer before the match and the referee's instructions must be specific in order to avoid confusion. The assistant referees must, for their part, fully appreciate the referee's supreme authority and accept his rulings without question should there be any difference of opinion amongst them. They must be supportive and never contradict his decisions.

The referee shall use the diagonal system of control if his assistant referees are neutral. If they are not neutral, he shall inform them which method he intends to use. He shall co-operate with his assistant referees on the following matters and tell them:

(a) the time by his watch;

(b) the side of the field which each assistant referee shall take in each half of the match;

(c) their duties prior to the start of the game, such as checking the appurtenances on the field;

(d) who shall be the senior assistant referee, if need be;

(e) their positioning during corner kicks;

(f) the sign denoting that he has noticed his assistant referee's signal but has overruled it;

(g) which detail in the throw-in shall be observed by the assistant referee and which by the referee. Some referees ask their assistant referees to watch out for foot faults while they themselves concentrate on hand faults.

Referees must not necessarily keep to one diagonal of the field of play. If the state of the ground or the weather demands a switch to the opposite diagonal, the referee shall indicate his intention to make such a change-over to the assistant referees, who shall immediately move to the other half of their line. One advantage of such a change in diagonal is that the surface of the ground next to the touch line will be less worn out because the whole length of the field will be utilized.

Other methods of co-operation may be used as long as all three officials are aware of them.

Co-operation Between Assistant Referees and Referee

When play has been stopped, the assistant referee shall assist the referee by signaling in the following manner for the following incidents:

1. *Offside.* The assistant referee shall lower his flag at full arm's length to the positions illustrated, and point across the field of play to indicate the spot from which the kick shall be taken. The only exception would be where the referee has decided to position himself to judge offside when play develops from a corner kick, penalty kick or free kick close to goal.

2. *Throw-in.* When the ball goes out of play over the touch line on his side of the field, the assistant referee shall indicate the direction of the throw. He shall also signal if the thrower's feet, at the moment of release of the ball, are incorrectly placed.

3. *Corner and goal kicks.* When the whole of the ball goes out of play over the goal line the assistant referee shall indicate whether a corner kick or goal kick shall be given.

4. *Goal.* When the referee indicates that a goal has been scored the assistant referee shall return quickly to his position towards the halfway line.

5. S*ubstitution.* When a substitution is to be made, the assistant referee nearest to the point of substitution shall attract the attention of the referee by illustration included in "Signals by the Assistant Referees" on page 140–141.

Law 7. If the assistant referee senses that the referee has not seen an infringment, he shall raise his flag high. If the referee stops play, the assistant referee shall indicate the direction of the free kick (direct or indirect), otherwise he shall lower his flag.

(Illustrations of signals by the assistant referees—see pages 137–141)

Signals by the Referee and Assistant Referees

The signals illustrated in this booklet have been approved by the International F.A. Board for use by registered referees of affiliated national associations.

Illustrations concerning signals by the referee are shown on pages 133–136. They are simple, universally in use, and well understood.

While it is not the duty of the referee to explain or mime any offense that has caused him to give a particular decision, there are times when a simple gesture or word of guidance can aid communication and contribute to greater understanding and more respect, to the mutual benefit of referee and players. Improving communication should be encouraged, but the exaggerated miming of offenses can be undignified and confusing and should not be used.

An indication by the referee of the point where a throw-in should be taken may well help prevent a player from taking a throw-in improperly. A call of "Play on, advantage" confirms to a player that the referee has not simply missed a foul, but has chosen to apply advantage. Even an indication that the ball was minutely deflected by its touching another player on its path across a touch line might be

---

helpful too in generating a greater understanding between referee and players. A better understanding will lead to more harmonious relationships.

All signals given by the referee should be simple, clear and instinctive. They should be designed to control the game efficiently and to ensure continuous play as far as possible; they are intended essentially to indicate what the next action in the game should be, not principally to justify that action.

An arm pointing to indicate a corner kick, goal kick or foul, and the direction in which it is to be taken, will normally be sufficient. The raised arm to indicate that a free kick is indirect is clearly understood, but if a player queries politely whether the award is a direct free kick or an indirect free kick, a helpful word from the referee, in addition to the appropriate signal, will lead to a better understanding in future.

The duties of the referee and assistant referees are set out briefly but clearly in the Laws of the Game, Laws 5 and 6.

The proper use of the whistle, voice and hand signals by the referee and the flags by the assistant referees should all assist understanding through clear communication.

Signals by the Referee

Play On – Advantage

Where the referee sees an offense but uses the "advantage," he shall indicate that play shall continue.

Penalty Kick

The referee clearly indicates the penalty mark, but there is no need to run towards it.

Signals by the Referee, cont.

Indirect Free Kick

This signal shall be maintained until the kick has been taken and retained until the ball has been played or touched by another player or goes out of play.

Direct Free Kick

The hand and arm clearly indicate the direction.

Signals by the Referee, cont.

Goal Kick

Signals by the Referee, cont.

Corner Kick

Caution or Expulsion

With the card system, the card shall be shown in the manner illustrated. The player's identity must be recorded at the same time.

Signals by the Assistant Referees

Offside

Flag held upright to indicate offside.

Offside

When the referee stops play, the assistant referee indicates the position on the far side of the field.

Signals by the Assistant Referees, cont.

Offside

Position near the center of the field.

Offside

Position on the near side of the field.

Signals by the Assistant Referees, cont.

Throw-in

Corner Kick (below)

The assistant referee may first need to signal that the ball has gone out of play if there is any doubt. He should also look at the referee in case he has already made his own decision, which may be different from the assistant referee's.

Signals by the Assistant Referees, cont.

Goal Kick

Substitution

Back view of the assistant
referee signaling to the
referee for a substitution
to be made.

Signals by the Assistant Referees, cont.

Substitution

Front view of the assistant referee signaling to the referee when a substitute is waiting at the lines.

Stay Involved with Soccer— Become a Referee

You may know how to play soccer, but do you know the Laws of the Game?

A great way to apply your knowledge and stay involved with the world's most popular sport is to become a soccer referee.

As the number of people playing soccer in the United States continues to grow at a rapid rate, the need for qualified referees and assistant referees also grows at all levels of play—recreational, youth, high school, college, amateur, and even professional.

U.S. Soccer undertook the responsibility in the early 1970s to develop programs for training a large number of referees. The training is conducted by qualified state referee instructors in a consistent manner throughout the nation. Referees are required to attend annual, advanced national training programs. American referees are playing an increasing role in CONCACAF matches and continue to get more and better appointments to work international matches. U.S. Soccer referee membership has been increasing steadily over the past decade.

There are 11 different levels for registered referees, ranging from local leagues and organizations to international competitions. Those select referees who attain a ranking from FIFA, the world governing body of soccer, are eligible to referee matches at any one of FIFA's world championships.

If you are interested in learning more about becoming a referee, please fill out the form below and your name will be forwarded to the appropriate referee administrator in your area, or call the U.S. Soccer Referee Department at 312/808-1300.Or, for more information, visit our website at www.ussoccer.com.

Name _____

Address _____

City _____

State_____ Zip Code_____

Phone _____